T0417629

Animals with Venom
Pit Viper

by Julie Murray

Dash!
LEVELED READERS
An Imprint of Abdo Zoom • abdobooks.com

1

Dash!
LEVELED READERS

Level 1 – Beginning
Short and simple sentences with familiar words or patterns for children who are beginning to understand how letters and sounds go together.

Level 2 – Emerging
Longer words and sentences with more complex language patterns for readers who are practicing common words and letter sounds.

Level 3 – Transitional
More developed language and vocabulary for readers who are becoming more independent.

THIS BOOK CONTAINS RECYCLED MATERIALS

abdobooks.com

Published by Abdo Zoom, a division of ABDO, PO Box 398166, Minneapolis, Minnesota 55439.
Copyright © 2021 by Abdo Consulting Group, Inc. International copyrights reserved in all countries.
No part of this book may be reproduced in any form without written permission from the publisher.
Dash!™ is a trademark and logo of Abdo Zoom.

Printed in the United States of America, North Mankato, Minnesota.
052020
092020

Photo Credits: Alamy, iStock, Shutterstock
Production Contributors: Kenny Abdo, Jennie Forsberg, Grace Hansen, John Hansen
Design Contributors: Dorothy Toth, Neil Klinepier, Candice Keimig

Library of Congress Control Number: 2019956185

Publisher's Cataloging in Publication Data

Names: Murray, Julie, author.
Title: Pit viper / by Julie Murray
Description: Minneapolis, Minnesota : Abdo Zoom, 2021 | Series: Animals with venom | Includes online resources and index.
Identifiers: ISBN 9781098221065 (lib. bdg.) | ISBN 9781644944011 (pbk.) | ISBN 9781098222048 (ebook) | ISBN 9781098222536 (Read-to-Me ebook)
Subjects: LCSH: Pit vipers--Juvenile literature. | Snakes--Juvenile literature. | Poisonous animals--Juvenile literature. | Poisonous snakes--Venom--Juvenile literature. | Bites and stings--Juvenile literature.
Classification: DDC 591.69--dc23

Table of Contents

Pit Viper

Pit vipers are found around the world. Most live in places that are warm.

They are named for their heat-sensing **pits**. These help them find **prey**.

Pit vipers have long **fangs**.
The fangs have **venom**.

Pit vipers hunt at night. They eat frogs, lizards, and birds.

Pit vipers bite their **prey**. The **venom** slowly kills the prey.

All rattlesnakes are pit vipers. Their rattles warn of danger!

Copperheads are pit vipers too. They live in the US. They got their name from the color of their scales.

Cottonmouths live on land.
They also live in the water.

The bushmaster is the biggest kind of pit viper. It can be 12 feet (3.7 m) long!

More Facts

- There are more than 100 different kinds of pit vipers.

- Up to 8,000 people are bitten by venomous snakes in the US each year.

- Of the 8,000 people bitten each year, around 5 people die.

Glossary

fang – a long, pointed tooth used to inject poison.

pit – a temperature-sensitive organ located on each side of the head midway between each nostril and eye. It helps the snake "see" heat images of warm-blooded prey.

prey – an animal that is hunted and eaten by another animal.

venom – a poison that certain animals make.

Index

Online Resources

Booklinks
NONFICTION NETWORK
FREE! ONLINE NONFICTION RESOURCES

To learn more about pit vipers, please visit **abdobooklinks.com** or scan this QR code. These links are routinely monitored and updated to provide the most current information available.